Homing

Homing

poems

Alison Hicks

Sheila-Na-Gig Editions

Homing © 2024 Alison Hicks
Cover art: Catherine Bancroft, *Deer*, Mixed Media
Author photo: by Alison Hicks
ISBN: 978-1-962405-11-9
Library of Congress Control Number: 2024946195

Sheila-Na-Gig Editions
Russell, KY
Hayley Mitchell Haugen, Editor
www.sheilanagigblog.com

ACKNOWLEDGMENTS

The author is grateful to the publications in which the following poems have appeared, sometimes in slightly different form:

After the Pause: "Toward Protection of the Colony," "Poem with a Line by Carolyn Forché"
Boomer LitMag: "Saguaro National Monument"
Brief Wilderness: "Equinox in Plaguetime," "Swing"
Carbon Culture Review: "Poem for a New Year"
Cortland Review: "The Wanderer"
ELM: "Alterations"
Figure 1: "The Ask"
Glassworks: "Where I'm From There Are Few Children"
Grist: A Journal of the Literary Arts: "Love Poem"
Isele Magazine: "Gone, Gone, to the Further Shore"
Journal of Undiscovered Poets: "Red Clay"
Medicine and Meaning: "Field Notebook at Tinicum"
Midwest Quarterly: "Petawawa" and "Night-Blooming Jasmine Is Not the Same as Jasmine" from "Homing" sequence
Mulberry Literary: "Line," "Nightscape"
New American Writing: "Flower of the Field"
Open Arts Forum: "Who Will Find Us?" from "Homing" sequence, "Three Doors"
Pennsylvania English: "Marriage"
Poydras Review: "Lessons"
Press Pause: "Bright Angel"
Roi Fainéant: "This was California"
Saint Katherine Review: "Voice"
SLAB: "The Party"
Slant: A Journal of Poetry: "Something Joyful in the Scent"
Sliver of Stone: "Home"
Smartish Pace: "Debriefing with an Archangel"
Synkroniciti: "Hill Reservoir," "Teachers" from "Homing" sequence
The Citron Review: "Lives of Truffles" from "Homing" sequence

The Courtship of Winds: "280 Main Street"
The Opiate: "Aubade with Washcloth and Migraine"
The Phoenix: "I Would Not Marry and Have Children"
The Virginia Normal: "Mountain Ash"
Visitant Lit: "At 45" (under title "The Poet at 45")
Vox Poetica: "Place of Seasons" (under title "Where I Come
    From")
Wild Roof Journal: "Hope," "Channel"
Willows Wept Review: "The Errand"

"Debriefing with an Archangel" was a finalist for the 2021
Beullah Rose Prize from *Smartish Pace*

My gratitude to Leonard Gontarek and the Saturday Osage
Poets, who saw early drafts of these poems; Trudy Hale of The
Porches Writing Retreat, where various drafts of this book were
put together; and Amy Small-McKinney and Catherine
Bancroft, who offered comments and helpful guidance on that
first draft of the book. An additional call-out to Catherine for
contributing the cover image and providing proofreading
assistance.

Thanks also to Hayley Mitchell Haugen of Sheila-Na-Gig Editions
for selecting this book for publication and for her helpful editorial
comments. I am proud to be counted among Sheila-Na-Gig
authors.

And as always, my husband Charles Greifenstein and my son
Jeremy Greifenstein (the archivist and the naturalist, respectively.)

For the Archivist and the Naturalist

CONTENTS

I.

II.

III.

I.

VOICE

Even when I couldn't make out the exact words,
I attended, the way you listen to water,
not comprehending but relishing the flow.

More muscular than whisper,
dropping in volume and pitch
at its most vulnerable, as if drawing a curtain.
The more desperate to hear
what request for repetition could only dissipate.

There was humor there, wryness,
even crusted over with anger, gentleness
that made me ache.

How could I tell?
Training my ear and straining
though fatigue pulled at my eyelids.

What I really wanted was something
the voice pointed to, a way to rest
beyond the words,
though I would never give up listening.

It was a path, and I followed the logic
of its aesthetic up and down, rounded vowels,
palatals and sibilants, to its natural conclusion.

THE PARTY

No mystery we are a mystery to ourselves,
bottle we cannot drink from, only pour for others,
track the play of florals, musk, and fruit
in animation of faces and voices.

Some pour extravagantly, overflowing glasses
splashing onto white shirts.
Others emit, measuring
from a source finite, unrefillable.

Who the wiser, the stain broadcasting its presence,
refusing bleach, the vessel
placing itself on a shelf as a work of art?
Both trying to make a statement while it's possible.

We don't know what happens once the bottle's empty,
the party's over, after guests have staggered back home,
and years later rave about the night,
clarity of stars seen from the bridge,

wine unlike any before or since,
sweeter and deeper, subtle.
It went down easily as our blood.

GIFTS OF THE MEDITERRANEAN

I. Evidence

A beach of green stones

A freezer of ice-cream sandwiches in a hotel driveway

A blow-up flotation ring with a duck head I called Paprika

A living sponge—the first I'd seen

A bamboo model raft my father called Kon-Tiki

A rough crossing in which everyone was sick

II. Myths

When the waves were rough and made noise at night
my father said that Poseidon was angry.

He'd been in the Navy so knew about Poseidon and his moods.

My mother told about the competition between Athena and Poseidon.

Poseidon struck a rock with his trident and water came out.
Salty, not good to drink. Athena planted an olive branch.
Her gift deemed the more valuable, the city named after her.
Maybe one reason Poseidon was always getting angry.

III. Offerings

We ate breakfast on the terrace above the sea.

Toast with honey. Bees swarmed the pot, utensils, the slices
in our hands. Impossible to eat without getting
a mouthful of bees.

The waiter brought out a wooden contraption with a wire cage,
bowed and disappeared.
The bee trap sat on the brightly painted table, ignored by the bees.
We abandoned breakfast to them.

The best thing for seasickness was Melba toast, my father said.

> Small pieces, eaten very slowly.
> I scraped the edge with my teeth.

We found *Kon-Tiki* on a rock at the end of a beach.

> I sailed it every time we swam.
> Standing chest-high in the water, holding its string,
> watching it ride up and down the waves.

When it was time to leave the country, we put the raft on a rock

> for the next person to find,
> or for Poseidon to drag down to the sea floor,
> cover with sand as he has other shipwrecks.

EUSTON STATION, 1965

Lights burn halos in the night.
The glare stays in my eyes when I look down:
my hand in my mother's, flow of travelers around us.
The train waits, a stretched-out animal, panting,
curving out of sight.

My father is going to Dublin,
the word rolls reverently from my parents' mouths.
My mother and I only coming this far.
I am as tall as the wheels with their rusty dust.
From underneath, a hiss and groan.

My father picks me up.
I stare into a pane, glossy streaks
like the patterns that appear when I close my eyes.
He kisses me, puts me down.

That's all there is, this threadbare, see-through scrap of memory,
rising like the steam from the bath my mother will run
in the room at the end of hall with the claw-foot tub,
the smell of Yardley English Lavender. *A cake*, she calls it,
        a cake of soap,
as if you could eat it.

WHERE I'M FROM THERE ARE FEW CHILDREN

Men with beards lean on the back of chairs, glass in one hand,
the other in the air conducting the response,
while women dressed in long, swingy prints slink through
bearing casseroles, brown stews of indeterminate ingredients.
Baskets of bread set on large wooden tables
between pillar candles that burn brightly, then sink
into their pools of wax, inside houses where bookshelves rise.

After gleaning what appears edible, I am free to read the titles,
wander through bedrooms piled with coats,
take inventory of bathroom cabinets, checking in mirrors
to see if they show me at unimaginable, unattainable ages.

When there are children, they group in hard knots,
unwilling to be pried apart, have in-jokes and speak
about things I've never heard of. They complain I am too quiet.
When they play dodge ball in the driveway before dark,
I discover I don't even have to move, that's how much
they aren't aiming at me. Someone says, *Hey, she doesn't know
how to play*. Pointless to jump when I don't have to.

Back inside, voices braid in a drone. I find some corner
to lay my head until I am awakened, coats pulled off
and onto me, escorted into the winter night. It always feels
like January or February, beginning of a new year.
I never feel any bigger.

280 MAIN STREET

I grew up in the town she lived in —
was led with school groups to her room —
desk — bed with coverlet — white —
dress preserved on a standing hanger —

The younger boy of the family
that occupied the house those days —
parts visitors were not allowed to go —
was my age — I climbed

with him and the girl from across our street
to the cupola — where wasps flew lazily
above our heads — landing
in corners of the glass —

The soul acquainted with the fellow in the grass
selected her own society
then shut the door — the nobody who wouldn't
stop for death and asked if you were, too.

Wren's footprints on the backs of bills
and envelopes — copied out — folded —
bound into fascicles.

We were told she loved the children
of the town — let down baskets
of gingerbread on a rope from her bedroom window
facing Main Street and the Congregational Church —

When we moved out of town
I passed her house twice a day
going down and up Pelham hill.

MOUNTAIN ASH

The mountain ash grew next to the stone wall.
This wouldn't matter except that everyone remembers a tree
from childhood. I had a book about a doll
carved from a piece of mountain ash
carried for luck by an old peddler
who makes the doll for a little girl
to thank her family for sheltering him
during a snowstorm in Maine.
Odd pinnate leaves, white flowers, red berries in fall,
smaller and lither than the maples and oaks and pines
that thrived through the winter it too survived.

I had a wooden doll, carved from a single block
of brown wood, two braids coiled at the base of her neck,
that came to me through my mother from the grandmother
I saw only once, in a hospital bed in Philadelphia.
Her disease turned her body into wood.
She could wiggle her nose. Like a bunny, she said.
When my mother told me that she'd gone to meet God,
I pictured her rolling up the hill to the stand of pines
outside our old apartment in a wheelchair.
When I told my mother, years later, she said,
Did I really say that? And then,
That's what she would have wanted me to say.

There were other trees:
the maple in the upper meadow, next to the woodpile,
from which my father hung a rope and a board
to make me a swing. The white oak with its shaggy bark
that hung out over the driveway. The lilacs
that reached to my second-story windows.

Unlike these, by whose growth you could measure time,
the mountain ash never seemed to change in size or proportion.

It wasn't a tree I played in or climbed on.
In Europe it was said to ward off witches
and the pentagram on the shaft of its berries to bring good luck.
I don't know what happened to the doll
when my parents packed up the house.

None of this would matter, except that
things made of wood have qualities of trees,
breathe, absorb, and release,
offer up fruit for birds and small mammals.

THIS WAS CALIFORNIA

My grandmother's house had two half-doors,
Dutch doors they called them.
The top unlatched from the bottom,
swung open, you could stick your head
out. Indoors mixing with sun
burning through fog,
eucalyptus, damp bricks of the patio.
Redwood boxes of fuchsias,
little explosions of red, pink, purple.
Unable to survive a freeze, I knew,
or being brought indoors, I learned
when I hung a basket on our porch
for a summer back east. They die
without the movement of air across the skin.

EUCALYPTUS

Enormous peeling rolls of bark, skinny leaves
I mixed in a bowl and fed to the stuffed koala
I took everywhere, tucked in my armpit. On the road
to the beach my mother slipped
on the three-sided pods we called buds, blood
running down her leg. Gone now,
taken out in the '80s, as the invasives they were,
like us, only they lived there all year, for many years,
condemned along with the ice plant
that covered nearly every embankment. Still smell
them, a reflex. My grandmother's salt-and-pepper
schnauzer smelled like the beach, piles of washed-up
kelp, floats I'd jump on to pop. Without the trees,
room for a path, no need to walk on the side
of the road where buds collected,
roots pushed against edges of asphalt. Cars
came fast around the curves, still do.

THE GLASS EXTINGUISHER

Teardrop shape, bigger than a lightbulb,
hanging eye-level on a rack opposite the back stairs.
Black-and-white label, three figures, flames in the background.
Too fragile for the job — it couldn't have held more than two cups,
hardly enough for a small fire.
My friend Sally would stand at the top of the stairs
studying the ways, according to the label, it could be employed:
throwing, sprinkling, squirting,
consumed by the question, how could you squirt glass?

I'd been for a time afraid of fire.
I couldn't admit to my parents
every night I lay down with conflagrations.
Could not bear them
telling me I was safe, in no danger, there was and would be no fire.
When I finally confessed,
to a babysitter, listened to the same reassurances,
confession worked like it was supposed to:
a large bird disturbed from its perch, fear
unfolded, took flight.

The liquid inside the creepy extinguisher
was carbon tetrachloride.
It works by vaporizing over the burning,
sealing it from oxygen.
Toxic, a probable carcinogen —
nothing you'd want near a fire.
Squirting happened when heat struck
the liquid, shot it out the glass.

THE WANDERER

A storm has brought down the last of the leaves.
Drudgery settles over the bare hillside.
Your mother brings home a paperback,
faded cover, browning edges.

You're fifteen, the same age as the narrator,
as primed for the story as he is: château in the woods
doors and windows thrown open blazing light,
men and women arriving in costume.

They pull him inside, dress him in a silk vest and mask.
He wanders through rooms as if he's dreamed them.
There is dancing and they let him dance.
A young woman playing the piano tells him her name.

The map he draws from memory does not show the way back.

Years of French and you never read it in the original.
Le Grand Meaulnes. As if what traveled page to mind
might be undone.

LESSONS

Let yourself in, wait in the living room.
The cat knows the orange couch shows off his tortoiseshell fur.

Photo on the wall: your teacher laughing in a canoe.
When she calls, pick up your instrument.

Grand piano, window, two chairs facing the bookcase.
She on the right, you on the left.

Where to put your fingers,
how to move the bow.

Her voice and the cello sound.
She writes instructions for practice in a clear hand.

You can never be her, but if you could choose
to spend your life inside this room, you would.

THE FRENCH CALL IT L'ÂME

They brought the cellos out, one after another,
standing over me, correcting my accidentals.
I chose one with dark varnish
hairline scars on the top, bookmatched back.

I set it in its case in the cold car
while we went to dinner before the long ride home.
In the morning, I lifted it across my knees,
something solid rolled down inside.

In tears I called my teacher to confess I'd broken it.
She sent me to a man who slipped an S-shaped tool
through the f-hole, grabbed the loose soundpost
with a sharp-pointed star, set it underneath the bridge,

ends flush against top and back, then repositioned,
searching for the place the soul would sound.

AUBADE WITH WASHCLOTH AND MIGRAINE

I.

Washing my face on winter mornings,
staring into the mirror over the sink,
I'd think of other kids, all over town,
up and doing the same things:
getting dressed, going downstairs for breakfast.
I'd catch the bus at the corner
about the time the sun would appear,
mist rising off Hawley Reservoir.

II.

As if I just remembered
a fact forgotten in the hours of sleep,
something awful was going to happen
that I should fear and prepare for.

III.

Dream turning slowly
into a message of pain.
Reeling out of bed, catching on the dresser,
hands that have turned into mitts,
peel the pill from its silver backing.
My head moves into dawn,
filling with snow.

ALTERATIONS

I learned the hemstitch from necessity:
my mother and I, short for standardized sizes,
working though a pile of pants and skirts
in front of the TV.

The most pleasurable part of the labor—
after the trying on, the rough marking,
the measuring, folding and cutting,
pinning and ironing—

only then could the threaded needle
be slipped through two or three
of the outer fabric's threads.
A sleight of hand,

along with my mother's example,
I quit when I put away the skirts and dresses.
Nobody hemmed jeans.
Bottoms grew ragged and caught

under the heels of clogs or hiking boots.
An aesthetic I embraced as *wabi-sabi*,
before I knew there was a name for it.
She continued to bring me finds

from estate sales and thrift shops,
aging eyesight blind to stains.
Even to those gifts bought new, at full price,
I was at best indifferent, at worst hostile.

She took it well, accepted the complaint,
My mother's always buying me clothes,
meant to sound ridiculous,
joke to provoke friends' laughter.

It was the truth, I did resent
her giving me what she'd always wanted,
worldly goods for which I was now custodian,
pressing on me choices I'd rather avoid.

At fourteen, my son works in the third-floor room
we renovated for him.
Clothes, athletic equipment, textbooks, sheet music
disrupt the Persian rug's reds.

Music stand, cracked cake of rosin,
viola, and shoulder rest half out of the case.
In afternoon light, a still life I can almost choose to see.
He complains we have yet to put in blinds.

HILL RESERVOIR

The last day of the year,
my father and I walked to the reservoir
down the dirt road behind the church.
Heat radiated up legs to skin, sweat gathering at my back.
We turned into the rise: steps of the chute through snatches of pine.
The dog bounded through drifts, waiting at the clearing.
The sun skimmed the tree line on the other shore.
A sapling sprouted from the tower's crumbling top.

It was not the Quabbin,
below which three towns lay sunk.
As far as we knew, it had no name;
no ghosts lay beneath its ice.
All the time we were standing there, breath fogging air,
where we couldn't see, water was moving,
layers falling, rising, cooling, and dropping,
passing quietly over fish hugging the bottom.

SWIFT VALLEY ELEGY

The best way to the towns is to follow the fish.

Underneath the reservoir, the river flows in its old bed.

Seventy feet down, dumps along its banks eroded: bottles, crockery,
iron machinery from the turn of the twentieth century.

Mussels, sponges, polycheate worms: survivors from the lakes the
valley was known for.

The rest barren as when they finished clearing, some 80 years ago.

Dana, Enfield, Prescott, Greenwich.

The present floods the past, the past runs in its veins.

You cannot get to it by thinking. You cannot get to it by grasping.

The clearing took twelve years. At the depth of the Great Depression,
men came in from Ware and Springfield

tore down buildings, pulled up tracks, removed bodies from thirty-
four cemeteries.

The valley on fire for months.

Enfield held a ball, played "Auld Lang Syne," dissolved at midnight.

Inundation took seven years.

Twenty-nine square miles covered by four hundred twelve billion
gallons.

Twenty-five hundred exiled.

You cannot get to it by not thinking. You cannot get to it by not grasping

Old roads lead into water. Their paths can be traced from the air.

SWING

My father made me a swing.
In the upper meadow, above the stone wall
below the edge of the woods.

He pulled rope that lasted through my childhood
over the limb of a maple,
passed the ends through holes
in either end of a sanded board and knotted them.

Didn't rot through until I was home from college,
trying to figure out how to do what I wanted to do,
fit into the inhospitable world
that in the end I had to leave home for.

Those lonely, uncertain years I want to toss
as far away as I can, my son carries back,
dog with a stick in its mouth, wagging its tail,
nudging my leg to make me throw again.

II.

PLACE OF SEASONS

Mixed forest, evergreens and hardwoods.
Where sugar maples turn orange and red, whose sap,
collected in spring, boiled down, is poured hot onto snow.

Farmhouse that had been a tavern,
on the road to a town now sunk beneath a reservoir.
No heat upstairs, only what rose.

Journeys to warmer places, tent in the desert,
sun setting below raised arms of saguaros,
sips from a thermos of mulled wine.

Then back to granite and smell of leaf-litter.
A warming planet, what that means:
lesser snows, greater rains, drought, flood, disaster.

I've stretched my body out on the Canadian Shield.
I've lost the trail many times, then found it,
or maybe another one.

I WOULD NOT MARRY OR HAVE CHILDREN

I was going to live in the woods by a stream,
sleep on a pine-needle mattress in a house made of sticks.
Dance, paint, make things from wood with my hands,
crouch by a tree, write observations in a notebook.

I chased talent, never catching up.
I wanted to live with the musician,
make love with the scientist.
Trained as a novelist till plot undid me.

I married the librarian, the archivist
conserving letters from brilliant minds
for the future to unseal.
I had a child, watched him grow
into the naturalist I did not become.

I thought about hiking the Appalachian or Pacific Coast Trails.
Still infatuated with openings.
If I lost everything, I could join the Buddhist monastery,
shave my head, sit zazen, study the sutras.

No ceremony necessary.
Words always part of it.
For better or worse I accept my hand.

HOME

is the place the wasps come in.
You have no choice but to let them.
Buzzing the ceiling, flying high
when they need to fly low. Guide

them out the screen if you can,
goose them with a paper when they land.
Home is the earring with the missing stone
the hole you probe, wondering what will fit

in the space and where the lost piece is.
The dog who went over the fence
not by plan but chance, paws on top
and feeling it give, giving in to it.

Mice who find their way in
to live through the winter—
and who doesn't have
to live through a winter

of some sort or another?
It is the lover who left
and then came back,
unable to decide which is best.

The chipped glass marble buried in the dirt,
it catches your eye as you wait
on the corner with the runaway dog.

NORTH MANITOU

The Lake has been dropping, wrecks breach the surface.

We couldn't see for fog, the buoy brayed all night.
Morning we stepped out into Great blue,
walked the beach to a sand cliff pocked with holes,
swallows darting in and out, split tails ruddering above us,
calling their business, while backed-up lakers,
hulks on the horizon, made time
grinding engines through the straits.

Mishe-Mokwa the bear, Anishinaabe legend,
swam across Lake Michigan to escape a forest fire,
waits on the shore for her drowned cubs.

Mother in me stretched out waiting to be formed,
sand collecting along my flank.

AT 45

My son winding up to hit a ball off a tee,
I was crawling out of older motherhood
the way you back out of the tent or debark from a canoe.
Adding distance between myself and the scattered contents
of a diaper bag, trailing Cheerios, wipes, fruit roll-ups,
as gingerly as my son charged exuberant in a growing body,
I stepped into my office, where I'd relocated everything
that couldn't be lost or torn or shredded,
shut behind me the door of the room from which I'd once sought escape,
carrying the notebook downstairs to the chair, outside to the sun.
Only now my eyes were on the door as if I was escaping
by cornering myself in here, backs of legs hitting the chair
that rose up to catch me, the desk that offered up its surface
to a hand that started out small and neat, becoming bigger and more unruly
the way language does when it gets worked up and no one's looking,
words weaving in and out, no more pretense of staying between the lines,
ignoring stoplights and signs, stripping gears coming out of the gate,
accelerating on straightaways, leaning into turns.

MARRIAGE

You cook dinner, I do the dishes.
It wasn't that way when we started, but so it became,
ritual we fell into. You chop parsley and cilantro,
fold flavor into the sauce, calculate cooking time for the bird.
I don gloves, plunge hands into warm water,
let my mind float away on suds.

Labor that is divided is blessed
with the task of weighing: what equals what.
Art, not science, managed by instinct and feel
and by how much we are willing to argue about it.

We used to look in horror at those couples
together so long they might as well have been fused,
or who carp at each other's vulnerabilities all day for sport.
I hate to say it, but did we think there was a viable alternative,
barring death or divorce? Were we going to stay twenty-four and
thirty-one forever?

A woman who contracted Lyme disease—not once, but twice—
would still go out, in permethrin-soaked clothing and netted jacket,
searching for a firefly who flashes blue.
If wanting more awe is a kind of greed, she wrote, *I was greedy.*

Had we been two full years together when we drove to Organ Pipe,
on the Mexican border, to see Halley's Comet?
We parked your truck on a hillside and watched.
I leaned against your shoulder and slept until sunlight.

In the Santa Ritas, we went in search of elegant trogons
at the northernmost point of their migration.
I didn't expect to see them, but down by the stream,
we heard the hoarse calls, a nagging clearing of the throat,
through binoculars followed flights of red and copper-green.

We painted the back stairs terra-cotta and yellow,
listening on the radio to a ball game our team was losing.
I laid my back along the ground to reach the underside of the facing.
You never wanted an old house, you said after we bought the place.
You'll always have something to do, my father said.

Each discovery reminded me that more discoveries were possible.
If we've divided labor, we've also shared it.

THE ERRAND

I hadn't done the shopping in a while.
By the time I got to the store
they'd switched around the aisles.
And the items in the aisles,
toilet paper next to bread, spaghetti
mixed in with the candy.

The frozen foods were defrosting.
The flounder quietly breathing in the sand
at the bottom of the lobster tank.
I tried to remember what I'd been sent for,
something I should know, like a test,
figure out now I was here.

Beer? Something everyday like crackers,
or novel and hard to find like mead?
What we were missing at home?
What secret, nursed desires?
I walked slowly, with a hitch
since I threw out my hip.

Granny Smith apples in a pyramid
polished to high sheen.
There was a time we were lost in the wild
five days and five nights,
a survival chocolate bar between us.

The Holiday Inn was full,
the Miss Pennsylvania pageant in town.
We were dirty, in camping clothes, smelling of fire.
We took a room in a rundown motel.
Soft bed with a roof when the hard rain came.

We walked into the supermarket fluorescence
in slow motion, we were weak and the aisles long.

WON DHARMA

At dinner you take too much Kimchi.
What are you trying to prove?
You don't like pickled things as a rule.
Why not take a modest portion?
You put it on your plate then add more.
The flag of the ego flies.

After dinner you take a hike across the meadow.
A hawk rides high and speeds toward the trees.
Your son is flying to Frankfurt and then Rome.

On the wall in the meditation hall is a large circle, lit up.
You're still thinking about the hawk.
Your body says, *I hurt.* You have shut it out.

His father dropped him at the curb.
You would have parked and gone in.
From his latest text he's eating sushi in the airport with friends.

The dharma cat escorts you back to your dorm.
She prances ahead then sits,
springs up when you pass, sits again.
She wants something you don't know you can give.
Black and white fur thick—the cat in Japanese paintings.

At the door, you flirt: cat moving forward, you back.
Finally you slip in and she steps back.

The water is not as hot as it is at home,
but sufficient.

FIELD NOTEBOOK AT TINICUM

I could have used the set of traveling colors,
the brush with its barrel of water.
Winter hues:
ice-covered shallows,
dry stalks, ragged heads of phragmites,
sparrows that flew back and forth in the grove.
Plank bridge across the neck
where ice gives way to deeper water.
Quiet, considering the highway,
the train tracks, the airport,
walking here after the drop-off.
Squares of color arrayed,
shifting with sunset,
paper holding the rinse.

HEART OPERATION

The day of my father's, I was stuck
in a snowstorm. All flights canceled.
My cousin who lived on the West Coast called
after they were finished, my father in the ICU recovering.
I plugged the cell phone in downstairs, went to bed.

In the morning, a friend of my father's
speaking on the landline in the bedroom,
in a roundabout way,
as if there was something he was trying to get at
that he couldn't quite articulate.
Slowly I began to understand.

Not in so many words,
and neither could I form words to ask,
as if voicing it aloud would have made it
not only possible but true
so we both kept circling
while a tremor rose inside of me,
a cliff fell into the ocean, spray shot up,
plates collided, ground against each other,
and by the time I found a way to hang up,
my body was shaking.

My father's friend was wrong,
my father was not dead, then.
I found the message the surgeon left
on the cell phone in the middle of the night:
a clot, they'd had to open him up again.

Still, the earthquake had happened.
Four days later I would stand in the ICU
at the foot of a bed staring at the racks
of medications and tubes,
my father hallucinating the hospital was a ship,
and he back in the Navy.

FRIDAY AFTERNOON

Opal light in my office at the end of January,
the room cold, snow blowing sideways
through the limbs of the copper beech.
I want for a while no bills, to present none
and to owe none—
an end to negotiation of duties
to client, parent, house, and child,
to body and poetry, haggling
over costs and benefits,
to adding up,
what is worth what.

NIGHTSCAPE

There were dogs and stars
in the silence—strange thing:
dogs running, stretching front legs,
claws eating up earth, stars
popping into the clear night
like Matisse's cutouts.
Silhouettes of dogs in black.
I followed them over frozen ground.

It seemed important to convey,
stars and the dogs running,
only I didn't have the words,
they came afterwards.
In the moment, I had the paper,
movement of legs, and light
from the stars that was in the process
of reaching me.

GONE, GONE, TO THE FURTHER SHORE

Take an aphorism. Breathe the smell of cedar. Take diary,
make a drawing of it. One earring off, massage the lobe.
Forget where you left it, it will be a gift. Take your heart and
wring it out, make tea with the water. Hurry on to the next
thing. I don't know what to tell you. Jiggle the handle.
Kilometers. Lift your arms. Motion to the back. Nothing to
lose. Oppose your thumbs. Assume the position. Quarrel
with necessity, reason with longevity. Season lightly.
Remember the tea, made with your own heart-water? U
words: uvula, underwear, underwater. As King Lear
directed the Fool, unbutton here. A voracious appetite leaves
no stone untuned. Wisdom sits under a rock. Xeriscape. Is it
yours? What is the song of a zebra mussel?

*

Stare at the candle without blinking,
we were instructed,
until eyes flood with tears.
The word exactly: *flood*.
I focused on the flame. My eyes husks.
Finally, I blew it out. Eyes inflamed
as if I'd been crying.

*

A box of tea, a spoon, a dried-out acorn.
Use the spoon to dig an acorn grave.
Sprinkle tea over it.

*

He said the copper beech
might have two more good years.
The dog is eleven.
The lifespan for an American foxhound is 10-12 years.
I will have entered
a new phase of life.

THE ASK

1.

After I'd begged successfully for the job,
they made me a professional.
Easier to beg for an organization than for oneself,
but a decent mission statement is hard to come by.
All answers must be divisible by money.
I tend to mix up digits,
so they put me in charge of the words.

2.

What do you beg for, when no one is looking?
Why is it hard to ask for what you want?

3.

The dog places his paw on my thigh.
Flexes the webs between his claws,
not enough to hurt, just to keep a grip, and to make sure I notice,
looks sideways at the floor.
I am eating chicken.
He knows my heart as only a supplicant can.

BEGGING BOWL

For Victims of the Mass Shooting in Boulder, Colorado, March 22, 2021

We grieve their lives as we live our own:
flowers piled up by the King Soopers
and Umba, the boutique where one of the murdered worked.
Hand-painted rocks, stuffed toys, balloons.

The florist's busy hands,
wrists brushing against blooms,
the living stalks.
The artist balances rock on rock:
ten towers in a semicircle across Boulder Creek.

The eighteen-year-old music student from Minnesota
escaped when someone yelled, *Run,*
driving over the curb, not stopping until Louisville,
returns to play cello at the site.

We hiked the Lion's Lair trail, Sunshine Canyon up Mt. Sanitas
where you look down on the city,
the basin holding water and sky.

TALLGRASS

I do not believe in an afterlife but in a journey
that carries us from one state of being to another.
It happens in the time it takes to draw a breath,
that might be experienced as months or years.

Say we open eyes in tallgrass prairie,
like the grasslands in which our species was born:
Indian grass, bluestem, switchgrass, rosinweed, coneflower.
Bison, prairie dogs. Fires sweep through controlling growth of trees.

Wind blows us from this soft land into rising dryness.
Soapwood yucca, plains prickly pear, honey mesquite.
Shortgrass: blue grama, buffalo grass,
hailstorms, blizzards, tornadoes, drought.

As-sin-wati: Seen across the prairies, they look like a rocky mass.
Ascend cottonwood to one-seed juniper, ponderosa,
Douglas fir, quaking aspen, lodgepole
and bristlecone pine, blue spruce.

LINE

I drop my line   let it out
with its sinker   it goes down where I can't see
ripples out   from where it drops
I'm not looking for a fish   to catch by the lip
I will take a boot   a tire
whatever the river   gives up
the bottom cold and still   will not tell me
the riverbank   is silent
I am an interloper   they do not trust me
what have I done   to earn their trust
after all   I do not breathe water
I can only sit   here
with my line   quietly
let it float   above the depths

DEBRIEFING WITH AN ARCHANGEL

The envoy entered through my mouth.
Without looking up from my reading, I took a swig of beer.
Pain injected my left lower lip.
My hand went up, felt the streamlined body, flung it out.

My tongue found the harpoon
imbedded in flesh on my inner lip.
I pulled it out, held it neutralized in my hand:
dark pin with a bit of light at the end.

You doubt that an Archangel could take the shape of a flying insect,
read this as conceit?
Consider a bee's work: gathering, pollinating, the ferrying of messages.
Jacob wrestling with an unnamed opponent, from whom he extracts
    a blessing.

Through the rest of the night, the spot smarted and throbbed,
the space around it discolored,
swelling on the inside, visible when I pulled my lip down.

In your experience, don't the most important messages sting,
leave the greatest mark inside?
The blessing inexplicable, merging into the bloodstream,
rising to the tongue.

SOMETHING JOYFUL IN THE SCENT

The dog smells rain
wedges himself between chair and sill.
Just before, a hint of sea, of dill.

A COVID-19 survivor returned to the ICU.
He stood where his bed had been.
Remembered the digital clock.
The window, too, light coming through.

Hickory Creek in the Allegheny Forest,
I wanted to go back,
a place I got lost,
to figure out the way.

Summers in northern California
only twice made it all the way in.
Past cold and the breakers,
lifted by salt and swayed.

SAGUARO NATIONAL MONUMENT

A small wind rises up.
Creatures hiding from the day emerge:
birds winging cactus to cactus,
insects unburrow, drone in the air.

Orange and red leach,
shapes shortening in the drop-off.
Authority turning over
from sky to earth.

Eyes we can't see.
Hunting time: when things with legs
and even the giant saguaros may
rouse themselves and move around.

We train on the blossoming
of a star, and the others that follow,
air so thin they shower on us,
pass the thermos until the wine is gone.

Sand cool now under feet,
we turn to the city, our home
on a neon horizon.

III.

TOWARD PROTECTION OF THE COLONY

Let no one tell you you have no home on this earth.

Read books and people equally well.
Walk streets of cities, hike the backcountry, paddle lakes and rivers.
Lighten your step with discovery, gentle touch; pick up after yourself.

May friction make experience memorable.

Find work you enjoy. If it should pay, don't let that sap the joy.
On occasion lose yourself in it.

Gather with friends and strangers without risking your life or theirs:
believe this will happen again in your lifetime.

When you dive through blue the reef will still be there.

PETAWAWA

To get from Cedar to Catfish requires five portages upstream.
From the Brent store dock, the shoreline is unending green.
Point straight across, paddle toward the sound.

By the waterfall near the end of the second portage,
too excited for the path, the child slipped—
was he six years old, seven? The branch that caught him hardly older.
We pulled him up, trying not to think of death or injury.

On Narrowbag, a moose stood in the shallows,
dipping her nose for pondweed and lily, sodium-rich,
baying as her suckling calf butted into her.

We floated, in a midafternoon
when it seemed the sun would never move.
By the time we put into Catfish it had set.

In near-dark, we climbed to a campsite,
ate by candle lantern, sitting on a log.
The river speaking source to confluence,
where it empties into another body,
one giving way to another.

WHITE-THROATED SPARROW

Whistle, whistle, trill,
first note long and piercing.
We learned to listen for it:
Oh sweet Canada Canada

How such a small bird can throw sound.
Every campsite, it seemed, we'd hear one
among the wails and tremolos of loons,
sometimes at night a barred owl,
Who cooks for you, who cooks for you-all!
Once, we thought, a wolf howl fading.

Whistle, whistle, trill,
song of northern forests outside my window
where I've not heard it before.

As if we are in the tent,
traveling lake to lake,
eavesdropping on a world not ours.

HOMING

I. Lives of Truffles

Homing, it's called, when fungal hyphae attract other hyphae
fuse and branch to form a spreading, sensing net,
in the dark under our feet, where we don't care to look,
stitching roots and soil together.

Fluent in chemicals, mycorrhizal networks have no need of sun,
get sugar from tree roots they must partner with or die.
The underground fruit
produce scents that rise through earth,
penetrate senses of animals who live on the surface,
compelling enough to dig up and consume,
every bite packed with spores.

Through the subterranean mycelium spreads
feeding by touch, exploring,
its shifting shape carrying
its map and its history—
where it's been and where it's going—
meeting the world where it is, digesting.

II. Loons on Misty

Running on water is not enough,
a headwind is required
to lift a bird built for diving.

At the base of the lake
they line up.
Slapping feet and wings against water,
drawing air under wings.

Evolutionary design, like the human kind,
forced into trade-offs.
Wings too short for flying,
they flap from Canada to Florida shores.
Too heavy for air if one feather is missing.

III. *Two Tones Against Brick*

Baby shoe, white and blue, on a brick sidewalk.
Upright, as if waiting for a foot
to come along, insert itself into it.

Leather, expensive, the kind of shoe
a parent might re-trace steps to find.
The kind my son would have kicked off.

I was on my way to visit a friend whose husband had died.
My small foot too big.

A woman from grad school told me she would find
discarded arms and legs of dolls in streets and gutters.
They're everywhere once you start looking for them, she said.
Discarded baby shoe the closest I have come.

Like everyone, I am bewildered by time.
I do not seek to go back.
Whatever the age, the heart is held
in a nest of pain. A different pain for each age.

Through a tunnel on a towpath along a canal
I once hiked long enough so that in the middle
no light came in from either side.

Nothing for it but to keep walking.
My friend ahead of me,
I can make out her back in the dusk.

I'm afraid to reach the place she is passing.
I place a hand on the damp bricks
that make up the arch above me.

I worry for myself, for all of us,
how we will sleep.

IV. *Teachers*

I figured it out the year of the French trip,
the way she talked about him.
I didn't think how far it might have gone,
enough for me then to know she loved him.

I turned the intimation in my heart's light,
staring into it. Feeling protective and virtuous
keeping it to and for myself.

When he was fired, years after we'd graduated,
and another teacher too, *for the same reason*,
my informant said, not needing to name it.
Kind of a shame, she added, he *was*
a good teacher—she was right, he was.
The shock there'd been others.

My friend married another student on that trip.
Both French teachers now.
Was it possible he didn't know?

Maybe like me he'd held that knowledge for her
until it broke open over them,
sealing an intimacy no one else could touch.

The way you might hold a coat for someone,
until their arms are ready to slip through the sleeve.

V. Jasmine Is Not the Same as Night-Blooming Jasmine

You wake to the pain of who you are,
lines remembered rushing in:
a self you shed in sleep.

On stage you stumble
sword plunged into the belly of you,
waking to the pain.

Decisions you've made, actions taken
wrong, untrue
to the self emerging in your sleep.

This waking one's a mess you would not choose,
gnawing truth,
the pain of being you.

Not opening eyes, you grasp to return.
No. Awake, aware, nothing you can do:
step into the self you shed in sleep.

As morning continues,
it grows on you:
the pain you wake to, who you are,
skin of the self you'll shed tonight in sleep.

VI. Who Will Find Us?

I want a larger territory
than a screen and two fingers allow.
Give me maps
impossible to fold back correctly.
It would not frustrate me
that they never sit flat
bulge awkwardly
testifying to my inadequacy.

Let them unfold
propped up on the steering wheel
over your entire body in the driver's seat
encroach into the passenger side
provoking vigorous objection
sharp corners just missing eyes
as you try to find your location
or somewhere that you are seeking
in the pasture of white and green
and intersecting lines.

POEM FOR A NEW YEAR

A little burns off,
stage of a rocket, falling away.
What will be left at the end:
something I will have become.

Year to year, hard to feel a difference.
What is unnecessary burns like paper,
brightest and hottest, leaves a fragile ash.
The necessary low and glowing,
needs no further power.

What circling? Do we get to know?
How long does the coal hold fire,
until it, too, begins free fall?

THREE SHORT NARRATIVES

Touched
I can put words on a page or screen, move
them around — the most untouched-by-God
skill ever. Foot in front, brick on brick.
I do not understand.
How does God move through the slant of blinds
into the despair of an afternoon?

Song
For your thesis, the composition professor said,
don't write something pretty,
write about something that matters.
The student set to music a book of poems about miscarriage.
Twenty years ago, the professor said, when he heard it,
my wife and I — we,
we had a miscarriage.

Snowplow
Trough for salt and spreader on the back,
in front of our house. After the last snow, it showed up,
hasn't moved since. There have always been vehicles
on our street that do not belong to residents.
I watch their arrivals and departures,
cars and trucks in some form of dilapidation.
Never before a snowplow. The tags are valid through November.

HOPE

How we came to it, we did not know.
We were a long way from the ocean.
We walked for a long time.
We could not say why we kept going.
Lack of alternative, possibly.
We drank from a deep hole,
water cooled in earth.
There were tall trees with thick bark.
Needles softened our steps.
Then mountains, snow.
We descended to a coast.
Fish and fruit were plentiful, and we ate.
How we came to any of it less than clear.
We told stories that pretended to knowledge.
Everything we saw was full
of meaning beyond us.

POEM WITH A LINE BY CAROLYN FORCHÉ

It is light that wakes
after a night where sleep is hard to find.
Neglected medicines line up in orange canisters.

Already it is diffused across the sky.
July nearly August, heat-bleached
clouds and sky indistinguishable, fused.

A wedge falls through the window
onto the edge of the yellow chair,
the red blanket folded over its back.

Languages and cities lost.
Crane on the book cover, neck curved and pointing up
gray feathers parted like fingers.

Apartness gathers the music of solitude as if it were a glass viola.
Like film or video on a loop, it keeps unfolding.

BRIGHT ANGEL

Lights move all hours of summer nights toward the South Rim.
Hikers who've forgotten: it takes twice as long to come up.
Easy to laugh at fools who don't know when to turn around.
A canyon is the reverse of a mountain:
the hardest part comes last.

Having traveled far to get here, would you stop,
this close to the river that made the journey through the same rocks,
over more years than you can grasp?
Worth being a fool for, and how eager are you
to climb back to your life?

DRIVING HOME AT NIGHT AFTER LIGHT RAIN

Coming back from rehearsal,
where I'd worked to acquit myself well,
I passed a house with lights on in every room.

I wanted to stop and be taken up
into the ease of those windowsills.

I continued, cello lying like a body
in its coffin in the back.
Empty streets, my home a few miles away.

RED CLAY

I'd like to wake up to mountains,
red cliffs, smell of ponderosa.
City throwing a net over the valley.

Those chased from their lands, their homes,
bless them, keep their feet intact.
Everyone should have a mountain,

snow-peaked or green, a city to call theirs.
Let everyone be issued a stamp, a pass.
Everyone her sea, to sail on it.

LOVE POEM

All I have is what breaks over me:
desert summer, the garden dug from caliche.
Freak ears of corn with scattered kernels, eyes popping out
    from the cob.
Hairpin ride up Mt. Lemmon, saguaro flowers blooming in
    the night.
How I learned to hate teaching freshman English,
the job in the born-again bakery, offer coming in from the east,
me hardly out of my sneakers after my shift, you on a knee,
the U-Haul with the damper that kicked in whenever we got
    up to speed.
Apartment with ceilings too low to take a shirt off overhead.
Shots of whiskey for cold walks to hockey games.
I hold up to my spreading body clothes that no longer fit:
bust too small, armholes too tight, the zipper will not close.
In a more temperate zone, you turn earth, I turn words.
We have been fortunate in each other. Lizards sunned
    themselves on our fence.

AZALEAS

Blossoms spill upending,
ascension without presumption.
The lavender clematis,
without provocation.

CHANNEL

The lamp sends down a cone of light,
lifting me from night.
I require nothing
of myself, my mind.
No one awake to make demands.
No work lists, trying
to remember, scheduling, cross-checking.

Nothing assigned, reading nothing I should.
Watery eyes, pages blurring,
the world's bewildering ways.
Injustices remain, unspeakable.
I step into the current.
Little fishes, spots of bioluminescence.
My finger touches their backs.

FLOWER OF THE FIELD

If nothing were to change we would still have the rain.
The dog would still lift his nose to the window to register the scent.
The heart that changes its mind hourly will not become more constant.

The Rose of Sharon crowded by the prickly holly.
I slip my arm through cotton, shoes to walk outside, sweat in
    noonday sun.
The higher the pressure, the thicker the muscle required to move blood
    through a body.

I take out the cello, adjust the contraption to hold the endpin,
strip of wood with holes and two wire arms
placed under legs of a chair, to keep the instrument from slipping.

When a fifth is in tune, the two sounds smooth out like mud flats
when the sea has retreated. This is what you must try to hear.

If nothing were to change, everything would need to keep changing:
the boy to grow up and leave home, the dog to contract palsy
    in his hind legs.

We would still have the rain, in any case, the rose its share of sun.

TO AUGUST

Here in the northern hemisphere you are what we want
to hold July ripened
tomatoes zucchini split with juices hummingbirds
drinking nectar from Rose of Sharon nights
gaining on days radiating katydids cicadas
coaxing us to mountains & sea warm
lakes & rivers inviting afternoon naps clouds
piling on horizon thunder sheets
of rain on pavement steamy & muddy
runoff moonlight
hikes reading late staying
up for sunrise two
hours of brightening *take*
take it cannot
stay long
on the table

HOW TO WRITE ABOUT JOY

A bird outside the window
waits until dusk to sing
repeating long sharp cries
until it is dark.

I have yet to eat a persimmon.

In the season of open
windows admitting sound
arpeggios from a violin:
garden tended fingertip to string.

GARDEN

This is not scorched earth, policed by armies
of fertilizers, pesticides.
Rabbits and deer nibble at leaves.
Garden, fox den. Possums and raccoons have been known
to waddle through at night. Compost steams in the back corner.

Lip of water widens over rock.
Pool where trout hang, hiding from sun.
Downed fruit of orchards, visited by drunken bees.
Garden, my garden, from the first you have witnessed brutality.
What grows here has fought for its place.

Pull on crabgrass runners to reveal the slate path.
Ferns and pine, shady and spacious underneath,
where trees grow old, fall in time.
Food here for everyone, larvae and beetles on up.
The barred owl calls at dusk.

EQUINOX IN PLAGUETIME

Though the sun sets earlier and faster
colors in the late afternoon hold
a portion of light,
lanterns coming on at dusk.

The gardener who pried away
a summer vine
holds the broken end in dirty fingers,
root tunneling beyond reach.

Drones have been evicted from the hive.
Workers cover the queen, and her brood
feeds on honey and shimmies flight muscles
without moving wings.

THREE DOORS

—after "Three Times My Life Has Opened" *by Jane Hirshfield*

Fragrant grasses that covered me.

Packed earth by fire, tending.

Cone of streetlight, red leaves.
Slow walk with an aging dog,
morning or twilight, it is the same.

NOTES

Page 21: "280 Main Street"
Amherst, Massachusetts, address of Emily Dickinson
Homestead

Page 26: "The Glass Extinguisher"
The earliest glass "grenade" fire extinguishers dated from 1870
to 1910 and were handblown and patterned, attached to a wall
with a metal bracket, and filled with salt water. After the turn
of the century, a more industrial design prevailed, filled with
carbon tetrachloride (CTC). Exposure to CTC for more than
fifteen minutes can lead to respiratory, gastrointestinal, kidney,
thyroid, brain, and developmental problems. When CTC is
exposed to the heat of a fire, it can produce phosgene gas, a
chemical weapon used in WWII.

Page 27: "*The Wanderer*"
Lowell Bair's English translation of Alain Fournier's *Le Grand
Meaulnes* (Signet Classics, 1971).

Page 29: "The French Call It *L'Âme*"
The sound post of instruments in the violin family is called
l'âme (the soul) in French.

Page 34: "Swift Valley Elegy"
The Swift River was dammed and the towns of Dana, Enfield,
Prescott, and Greenwich were inundated to create the Quabbin
reservoir in western Massachusetts to provide drinking water
to the city of Boston. Construction began in 1936, filling
commenced in 1939, and was completed in 1946 when water
first flowed over the spillway.

Page 42: "North Manitou"
Island in Lake Michigan, part of Sleeping Bear Dunes National
Lakeshore. The area includes the Manitou Passage Underwater

Preserve, home to a number of shipwreck dive sites. Recently, dropping water levels in Lake Michigan have exposed greater portions of wrecks.

Page 44: "Marriage"
Information about the blue-flashing firefly and quotations are from "Show Blues," by Tamara Dean, *The American Scholar*, Autumn 2020.

Page 47: "Won Dharma"
Setting is Won Dharma Meditation and Retreat Center, Claverack, NY.

Page 48: "Field Notebook at Tinicum"
Setting is John Heinz National Wildlife Refuge at Tinicum, Philadelphia, PA.

Page 52: *"Gone, Gone to the Further Shore"*
Translation of the mantra at the end of the Heart Sutra, *Gate Gate Paragate Parasamgate.*

Page 54: "Begging Bowl"
Dedicated to the memory of the victims of the mass shooting at a King Soopers supermarket in Boulder, CO, March 22, 2021: Tralona "Lona" Bartkowiak, Suzanne Fountain, Teri Leiker, Kevin Mahoney, Lynn Murray, Rikki Olds, Neven Stanisic, Denny Strong, Eric Talley, and Jody Waters.

Page 55: "Tallgrass"
As-sin-wati is the Cree word for the Rocky Mountains. Full translation "Seen across the prairies, they look like a rocky mass."

Page 59: "Saguaro National Monument"
Now Saguaro National Park in Pima County outside Tucson, Arizona.

Page 64: "Petawawa"
A river in the Saint Lawrence River drainage basin in Renfrew County in eastern and northeastern Ontario, Canada. It is the only one of two major tributaries of the Ottawa to flow completely free. The name comes from Algonquinian for "where one hears a noise like this," referring to its many rapids. It rises in Ralph Bice Lake and flows through several lakes in Algonquin Provincial Park, entering the Ottawa River at the town of Petawawa.

Page 66: "Homing" sequence
"Lives of Truffles:" for information about truffles and fungal hyphae I am indebted to the fascinating book on the subject, *Entangled Life* by Merlin Sheldrake (Random House, 2020). "Loons on Misty:" Misty is a lake in Algonquin Provincial Park through which the Petawawa River flows.

Page 74: "Poem with a Line from Carolyn Forché"
"Apartness gathers the solitude as if it were a glass viola" from "Elegy for an Unknown Poet" in *The Lateness of the World* (Penguin, 2020.)

Page 75: "Bright Angel"
Hiking trail in Grand Canyon National Park, originating in Grand Canyon Village on the South Rim, descending 4,380 feet to the Colorado River.

Page 81: "Flower of the Field"
Matthew 6:28: "Consider the lilies of the field, how they grow; they toil not, neither do they spin" (King James version).

Page 86: "Three Doors"
"Three Times My Life Has Opened" by Jane Hirshfield in *Lives of the Heart* (HarperCollins, 1997).

Alison Hicks was awarded the 2021 Birdy Prize from Meadowlark Press for *Knowing Is a Branching Trail*. Previous collections are *You Who Took the Boat Out* and *Kiss*, a chapbook *Falling Dreams*, and a novella *Love: A Story of Images*. Her work has appeared in *Eclipse, Gargoyle, Permafrost,* and *Poet Lore,* among other literary magazines. She was named a finalist for the 2021 Beullah Rose prize from *Smartish Pace,* an Editor's Choice selection for the 2024 *Philadelphia Stories* National Poetry Prize, and nominated for a Pushcart Prize by *Green Hills Literary Lantern, Quartet Journal,* and *Nude Bruce Review*. She is founder of Greater Philadelphia Wordshop Studio, which offers community-based writing workshops.

Sheila-Na-Gig Editions